Easy, Simple BUT *Good Food*

© 2022 Rose Barnes-bey McLaurin. All Rights Reserved.

Easy, Simple but Good Food.
Copyright © 2022 All rights reserved – Rose Barnes-bey McLaurin

No portion of this book may be reproduced or transmitted in any form or by any means, graphic, electronic, or mechanical, including photocopying, recording, taping, or by information storage retrieval system without the written permission of the publisher.

Please direct all copyright inquiries to:
Kingdom Trailblazers
c/o Author Copyrights
Post Office Box 767
Flora, MS 39071

Hardback ISBN: ISBN: 979-8-9865905-0-9
Layout & Design: Kingdom Trailblazers Publishing
Printed in the United States.

DEDICATIONS

I dedicate this book to my kids. Never ever give up on your dreams.

MEET THE CHEF

Rose Barnes-bey McLaurin

Rose Barnes-bey McLaurin, also known as Rose, was born in Jamaica Queens, NY but reared in Jackson, MS. Rose never thought in a million years that she would become a Chef. When she was younger, she wanted to be a cartoonist, tattoo artist, and scientist but all of that changed at a young age of 14. That's when she started cooking and has been ever since.

She has twenty plus years in the culinary industry and has her own catering business. She has cooked and managed at some of the best restaurant around Jackson Metro Area. Cooking will forever be her passion!

@rozaykitchenmcvsbey2

TABLE OF CONTENTS

07
Cooking Tips

08
Kitchen Conversions

CHAPTER I — MAIN DISHES

10
Scallops with Cheddar Grits

11
Stuffed Lamb + Balsamic Glaze

13
White Fish + Orange Butter Sauce

14
Blackened Salmon

15
Mahi Mahi with a Creole Sauce

16
Savory Waffles

18
Scallops with Pomegranate Beurre Blanc

19
Creamy Blue Cheese Burger

20
Parmesan Crusted Fish with a Savory Waffle

22
Steak with Corn Maque Choux & Hollandaise Sauce

24
Fish with a Crawfish Cream Sauce

25
New Orleans BBQ Shrimp

27
Steak with Parmesan Cheese and Crabmeat

CHAPTER II – APPETIZERS

29
Stuffed Mushrooms

30
Stuffed Potato Skins

31
Strawberry Salsa

32
Shrimp Dip with Spicy Cream Cheese

33
Steak with Blue Cheese Bruschetta

CHAPTER III – SOUPS

35
Lobster Bisque

36
Chicken Noodles Soup

38
Steak and Potato Soup

39
Loaded Potato Soup

CHAPTER IV – VEGETABLES

41
Mixed Vegetables with with Italian Seasoning

42
Carrots + Brown Butter Garlic Sauce

43
Mixed Vegetables

45
Butternut Squash with Red Onions

46
Vegetable Medley

47
Squash, Zucchini & Green Onions

CHAPTER V – DESSERTS

49
Fruit Tart

50
Banana Pudding Cheesecake

51
Turtle Chocolate Caramel Cheesecake

53
Homemade Mint Oreo Ice Cream

54
Homemade Tiramisu Gelato

55
Apple Pecan Bread Pudding

CHAPTER VI – SALADS

57
Pasta Salad

58
Greek Salad

59
Fruit Salad

61
Caprese Salad

62
Potato Salad

CHAPTER VII – VEGAN DISHES

64
Vegan Chili

65
Vegan Fajitas

66
Sweet Potato Curry

67
Vegan Big Mac

69
Vegan Stir Fry

70
Vegan Breakfast Casserole

CHAPTER VIII – KIDS

72
Chicken Alfredo

73
Cheeseburger Casserole

74
Honey Hot Wings

76
Pizza Bread

77
Fruit Kabobs

78
Chicken and Waffles

CHAPTER IX – CAT FOOD

80
Chicken Liver and Salmon

81
Beef and Rice

83
Tuna and Oatmeal

84
Homemade Cat Nip

CHAPTER X – DOG FOOD

86
Chicken and Rice

87
Beef and Broccoli

89
Carrots and Turkey

90
Surf and Turf

91
Baked Treat

COOKING TIPS

1. Make sure you understand the recipe.

2. Make sure you can actually cook the recipe and if you can't, that's okay.

3. Feel free to make substitutions to the recipes for your life purposes.

4. Always choose the right plate, place the food in the right angles and always wipe the rim of the plate and garnish.

5. Cooking should be fun, easy and simple, not hard and miserable.

"There are 1,000 ways to cook something not just one!"

MAIN DISHES

SCALLOPS WITH CHEDDAR GRITS

| PREP : 5 MINS | COOK : 25 MINS | SERVES : 4 |

INGREDIENTS

- 1 tablespoon unsalted butter
- 1 cup cheddar cheese
- 3 cups grits
- ½ cup white wine
- 1 cup heavy cream
- ½ teaspoon minced garlic
- 1 cup all-purpose flour
- A pinch of parsley
- Salt and pepper to taste

Seared Scallops
- 1 tablespoon unsalted butter
- 1 pound jumbo scallops

INSTRUCTIONS

1. Grits: cook according to packaging instructions. Use salt and pepper to season to your liking. When grits are ready, add cheese and stir.

2. Seared Scallops: melt butter in a nonstick skillet. Wash and pat scallops dry (as much as possible), sprinkle with salt and pepper on each side, and add to pan. Cook scallops until they sizzle (if they do not sizzle, allow pan to get hotter). Shake gently to prevent sticking.

3. After 2-3 minutes, flip each scallop over. Cook scallops until they are brown. Transfer to a paper towel to absorb excess water.

4. In a small saucepan, melt the butter over medium heat. Do not let it sizzle or burn. Once it has melted, add the garlic, and cook for approximately 1 minute.

5. Add the flour, one tablespoon at a time, and whisk to prevent lumps. Add heavy cream, white wine, and garlic. Bring to a slight boil for 3-7 minutes. The sauce should be thick enough to stick to the back of the spoon.

6. Plate: Place cheese grits in a bowl or plate. Next, place the scallops on top and drizzle with the garlic cream sauce. Finally, garnish with parsley.

STUFFED LAMB + BALSAMIC GLAZE

PREP : 15 MINS | COOK : 1 HOUR | SERVES : 2

INGREDIENTS

- 2 racks of Lamb (French cut)
- 4 tablespoons canola Oil
- ½ teaspoon crushed garlic
- Salt and pepper to taste
- ½ cup bacon, cooked and finely chopped

Balsamic Glaze:
- ½ cup balsamic vinegar
- Salt and pepper to taste
- 3 teaspoon brown sugar
- 2 teaspoons honey
- 2 tablespoons flour

INSTRUCTIONS

1. Lambs should be clean and slit on the bottom. Do not cut through the whole rack to prevent ingredients from falling out on both sides.

2. Place bacon and garlic inside of the rack. Season the rack of lamb on both sides with the salt and pepper.

3. Pour the olive oil in a nonstick pan. Place the lamb (fat side to skillet) in the pan on medium heat. Allow the meat to sear to a golden brown on each side.

4. Preheat the oven to 365°. Place the rack of lamb in the oven in the same skillet. Cook for 10-30 minutes. If you would like it well-done, cook for another 10 minutes.

5. Remove the lamb from the oven and place on a cutting board for 10 minutes before cutting.

6. Balsamic Glaze:
Heat brown sugar, honey, balsamic vinegar, salt, and pepper in a small saucepan on medium heat. Bring sauce to a boil. Reduce heat and whisk in the flour, adding 1 tablespoon at a time to prevent lumps.

7. Let simmer for 20 minutes on low heat. Sauce should be thick when done.

8. Cut the rack of lambs into 4 bones. Place the lambs on a serving plate with your favorite rice and vegetables. Pour sauce over rack of lamb chops.

WHITE FISH + ORANGE BUTTER SAUCE

PREP : 8 MINS | COOK : 10 MINS | SERVES : 4

INGREDIENTS

- 4 pieces Flakey White Fish (your choice)
- 2 oranges
- ½ cup white wine (cooking)
- 2 teaspoons minced shallots
- ½ pound cold unsalted butter
- Salt and pepper to taste

INSTRUCTIONS

1. Cook fish to liking. Fish can be boiled, sautéed, or fried. When the fish is ready, place to the side.

2. Zest half of one orange and juice the remaining oranges. Put juice, zest, wine, and shallots in a medium saucepan on medium heat. Cook until it has a soupy texture.

3. Reduce heat, add butter (1 tablespoon at a time) and whisk. The butter is the only emulsifier for this sauce and if you add it slowly, the sauce will achieve a silky-smooth texture. Do not let the sauce boil. Add salt and pepper to taste.

4. Place the fish on a serving plate with your favorite vegetable or pasta and drizzle the sauce on top.

BLACKENED SALMON

PREP : 10 MINS | COOK : 10 MINS | SERVES : 4

INGREDIENTS

- 4 pieces Salmon fillets (skin on or off)
- 1 teaspoon paprika
- ½ teaspoon onion powder
- ½ teaspoon garlic powder
- ½ dried oregano
- 2 ½ tablespoons olive oil
- ½ teaspoon salt
- ½ teaspoon pepper

INSTRUCTIONS

1. Combine paprika, onion powder, garlic powder, oregano, salt, and pepper in a large bowl. Mix well.

2. Brush ½ tablespoon of olive oil on top of salmon fillets and sprinkle the spice mix on both sides of the salmon. In a nonstick skillet or cast-iron skillet, heat 2 tablespoons of olive oil over medium heat. Wait 2 minutes, then add the salmon fillets and cook for about 3-5 minutes. Cook to your liking. Reduce the heat to medium, flip the salmon fillets over and cook for another 3-4 minutes.

3. Place the salmon on a serving plate. Can be served with broccoli, rice, or pasta.

MAHI MAHI WITH A CREOLE SAUCE

| PREP : 8 MINS | COOK : 40 MINS | SERVES : 6 |

INGREDIENTS

- 4 pieces Mahi Mahi fillets (skin removed)
- 2 tablespoons unsalted butter
- 1 small onion, small diced
- 3 Roma tomatoes, small diced
- 1 teaspoon minced garlic
- 2 tablespoons dried thyme
- ½ green pepper, small diced
- ½ red pepper, small diced
- ½ cup chicken stock
- ½ teaspoon paprika
- ½ teaspoon salt
- ½ teaspoon black pepper
- ½ cup of heavy cream

INSTRUCTIONS

1. Season the fish with salt and pepper. Melt the butter in a large frying pan on medium heat. Sauté the fish for 3 minutes on each side and then remove.

2. Sauté the onion, garlic, tomatoes, and thyme for 5 minutes, stirring occasionally. Add the green and red pepper to the pan and cover with a lid. Cook on medium heat for 5 minutes and then add the heavy cream. Add the fish and simmer for 15 minutes in the sauce.

3. Place rice or vegetables on a plate, add the fish on top and then add the sauce.

SAVORY WAFFLES

PREP : 15 MINS | COOK : 10 MINS | SERVES : 5

INGREDIENTS

- 1 cup all-purpose flour
- 2 teaspoons baking powder
- 1 ½ teaspoons sugar
- ¼ teaspoon salt
- 1 large egg, lightly beaten
- ¾ cups & 2 tablespoons whole milk
- ¾ cups & 2 tablespoons whole milk
- ½ stick unsalted butter, melted
- Pan spray
- Waffle iron

INSTRUCTIONS

1. In a medium bowl, combine the flour, baking powder, sugar, and salt. Use a hand mixer on low speed to combine ingredients for 2 minutes.

2. Add the egg, milk, and melted butter. Blend well. Add any extra ingredients such as cheese, chives, chorizo, bacon, shredded carrots, or sweet potatoes, and blend well.

3. Spray both sides of the waffle maker and heat. Add 3 leveled ¼ scoops of waffle mix into preheated waffle maker. Cook for about 5-8 minutes or until waffles are a deep golden brown and crisp.

4. Remove from waffle maker and serve warm.

5. Place the waffle on a plate with your choice of sides.

*Shredded carrots or shredded sweet potatoes must always be drained of any extra liquid before adding.

Mahi Mahi with Creole Sauce

Blackened Salmon

SCALLOPS WITH POMEGRANATE BEURRE BLANC

PREP : 10 MINS | COOK : 30 MINS | SERVES : 4

INGREDIENTS

- 2 tablespoons & 1 teaspoon canola oil (separated)
- 2 tablespoons minced shallot
- ½ cup dry white wine
- 1 cup pomegranate juice
- 2 pounds fresh dry scallops
- 1 stick unsalted butter
- Salt and pepper to taste

INSTRUCTIONS

1. In a medium pan, sauté the shallots on medium heat. Add salt and pepper and cook until translucent.

2. Add the white wine and simmer over medium heat for about 3 minutes.

3. Add the pomegranate juice and continue to reduce until there is only about 1/3 cup liquid (about 15 minutes). Remove the pomegranate reduction from the heat. Slowly whisk in the butter until it is blended.

4. In a large pan, add the scallops with 2 tablespoons of canola oil over medium heat. Let the scallops sear for about two minutes on each side, without stirring. When done, they should be golden and caramelized.

5. Place your scallops on a serving dish. Add sauce on top. Can be served with pasta, rice, green beans, or spinach.

CREAMY BLUE CHEESE BURGER

PREP : 10 MINS | COOK : 10 MINS | SERVES : 4

INGREDIENTS

- 1 pound ground beef
- A pinch of kosher salt
- A pinch of black pepper
- 1 cup mayonnaise
- ½ cup sour cream
- 1 cup crumbled blue cheese
- Lettuce
- Tomatoes
- Hamburger pickle chips
- 4 sesame hamburger buns

INSTRUCTIONS

1. Season the ground beef and mold into a hamburger patty. Cook the ground beef in a pan on medium heat, to your liking.
2. Add the mayonnaise, sour cream, blue cheese, and a pinch of salt and pepper in a medium bowl. Stir.
3. Place your bun on the plate and rub the blue cheese sauce on the buns. Add your ground beef patties, toppings, and enjoy.

PARMESAN CRUSTED FISH WITH A SAVORY WAFFLE

| PREP : 8 MINS | COOK : 30 MINS | SERVES : 4 |

INGREDIENTS

- 1 cup Parmesan
- 1 cup canola oil
- 2 teaspoons paprika
- 1 cup flour
- A pinch of salt & pepper
- 4 fillets of favorite white fish
- Pan spray

Garlic cream sauce:

- 1/3 cup butter
- 1 tablespoon minced garlic
- 2 tablespoon all-purpose flour
- 2/3 cup heavy cream
- Salt and pepper to taste

Savory waffle:

- 1 cup green onions
- 2 cups all-purpose flour
- 2 teaspoons baking powder
- 1 teaspoon baking soda
- 1 teaspoon garlic salt
- Pinch of sugar
- 2 cups buttermilk
- 3 eggs
- ½ cup vegetable oil

INSTRUCTIONS

1. In a large skillet, add 1 cup of canola oil and warm on medium heat.

2. Place fish in a bowl and season with salt, pepper, and flour. Then place fish in the skillet and cook for 3 ½ minutes on each side.

3. Spray the baking sheet with the pan spray and add the fish. Place the parmesan cheese on top of the fish and place in the oven on 400° for 5-8 minutes.

4 In a large bowl, mix the flour, baking powder, baking soda, green onions, garlic salt, buttermilk, sugar, and eggs. Pour a ½ cup of waffle mix into the waffle maker.

5 In a small pot on medium heat, melt the butter. Then add the garlic and heavy cream, and whisk in the flour. Bring it to a slight boil.

6 Place the waffles on a plate, add fish, and top it off with the garlic cream sauce.

STEAK WITH CORN MAQUE CHOUX & HOLLANDAISE SAUCE

| PREP : 15 MINS | COOK : 1.5 HOUR | SERVES : 4 |

INGREDIENTS

- 4 - 6 ounce filet mignon

Corn maque:
- 2 tablespoons unsalted butter
- 1 onion, diced
- 1 green bell pepper, diced
- ½ teaspoon minced garlic
- 1 bag frozen sweet corn (14 to 16 ounce)
- 1 can petite diced tomatoes, drained
- ½ cup heavy cream
- A pinch of salt and pepper

Hollandaise sauce
- 4 large egg yolks
- 2 tablespoons lemon juice
- 1 pinch salt
- 1 pinch cayenne pepper
- ¼ cup unsalted butter, melted

INSTRUCTIONS

1. Steaks can be grilled, sautéed, or broiled. Cook to your liking.

2. **For the Corn Maque**
   In a large skillet, melt the butter over medium heat. Add the onions and peppers and cook until they are tender (about 5 minutes). Add the garlic. Stir frequently for 1 minute.

3. Add the corn, tomatoes, and heavy cream, and stir to combine. Add the salt and reduce the heat to a low simmer. Cook uncovered for 15 to 20 minutes, or until the corn is cooked through and most of the liquid has evaporated. Now add salt and pepper.

4. **Hollandaise Sauce**
   Whisk the egg yolks and lemon juice together in a medium, stainless-steel bowl until the mixture is thickened and doubled in volume.

5. Place the bowl over a saucepan containing barely-simmering water (or use a double boiler). The water should not touch the bottom of the bowl. Continue to whisk rapidly. Be careful not to let the eggs get too hot or they will scramble. Slowly drizzle in the melted butter and continue to whisk until the sauce is thickened and doubled in volume.

6. Remove from heat, whisk in cayenne, salt, and lemon juice. If the sauce gets too thick, whisk in a few drops of warm water before serving.

7. To plate, place corn masque choux on the bottom of the plate, then steak, and finally hollandaise sauce.

FISH WITH A CRAWFISH CREAM SAUCE

| PREP : 8 MINS | COOK : 30 MINS | SERVES : 4 |

INGREDIENTS

- 4 fillets fish (salmon, tilapia, cod, or redfish)
- 1 cup olive oil
- 1 yellow onion, small diced
- Cajun seasoning to taste
- 1 pound crawfish tails
- 1 cup roma tomatoes, small diced
- 1 tablespoon minced garlic
- 2 cups heavy cream
- ¼ cup chopped green onions

INSTRUCTIONS

1. Heat oil in a medium pan over medium heat. Add the yellow onions and Cajun seasoning. Add the crawfish, and cook for 2 minutes.

2. Add the tomatoes & garlic and cook for 3 minutes. Then add the heavy cream and bring to a boil.

3. Reduce heat to medium & simmer, stirring occasionally, until the cream thickens and reduces (about 6 to 8 minutes). Add the green onions. Set aside & keep warm.

4. Heat a large pan with remaining 1/4 cup olive oil over medium-high heat. Season fish with salt and pepper. Add fish to the pan & sear until fillets are golden brown (about 8 to 10 minutes). Remove & drain on paper towels.

5. Plate: place fish on a serving plate and pour crawfish sauce over fish.

NEW ORLEANS BBQ SHRIMP

PREP : 8 MINS | COOK : 15 MINS | SERVES : 5

INGREDIENTS

- 2 pounds peeled shrimp
- ½ stick butter
- ¼ cup Worcestershire sauce
- 2 bunches green onions, small chopped
- 2 bay leaves
- 1 tablespoon Creole Seasoning
- 1 teaspoon oregano
- 1 ½ teaspoons paprika
- ½ teaspoon black pepper
- ¼ teaspoon cayenne pepper
- 2 teaspoons garlic, minced
- 2 tablespoons lemon juice
- 2 lemons, sliced
- 1 box of grits
- 1 cup of cheddar cheese
- ¼ cup of olive oil

INSTRUCTIONS

1. In a medium pot, cook grits according to instructions on package. When grits are done, stir in cheese.
2. In a large skillet, add the olive oil and sauté the shrimp for 4-6 minutes, or until done.
3. Place remaining ingredients in the skillet with the shrimp and bring to a boil. Let simmer for 5 minutes.
4. Place cheddar grits in a bowl and spoon shrimp sauce on top.

White Fish + Orange Butter Sauce

Asparagus Pasta with Flounder

STEAK WITH PARMESAN CHEESE AND CRABMEAT

| PREP : 8 MINS | COOK : 15 MINS | SERVES : 5 |

INGREDIENTS

- 4 - 12 ounce ribeye
- 1 pound crabmeat
- 1 cup Parmesan cheese
- Salt and pepper to taste

INSTRUCTIONS

1. Steaks can be grilled, broiled, or sauteed. Cook to your liking.

2. Mix crabmeat and Parmesan cheese in a bowl together. Add salt and pepper.

3. After steaks are done, place crabmeat topping over steak and place in the oven (on broil) for 1-3 minutes, or until cheese becomes golden brown.

4. Now place steaks on a serving plate.

APPETIZERS

STUFFED MUSHROOMS

| PREP : 5 MINS | COOK : 30 MINS | SERVES : 8 |

INGREDIENTS

- 16 oz whole mushrooms
- 8 oz chive and onion cream cheese spread (room temperature)
- 3 cups Parmesan cheese
- A pinch of parsley

INSTRUCTIONS

1. Preheat your oven to 400°. Wash your mushrooms and remove the stems.

2. Take a spoonful of the cheese filling and fill each mushroom where the stem was. Place them cap-side down in your baking dish and bake for 17 minutes.

3. Take your mushrooms out and sprinkle the tops with the Parmesan cheese. Bake for another 5-10 minutes, or until the cheese becomes golden brown.

4. Now place on a serving plate and enjoy.

STUFFED POTATO SKINS

PREP : 10 MINS | COOK : 30 MINS | SERVES : 6

INGREDIENTS

- 4 large Idaho potatoes
- ¼ cup olive oil
- 2 tablespoons Parmesan cheese
- ½ teaspoon garlic powder
- ½ teaspoon paprika
- 1 cup of bacon, cooked and crumbled
- ½ cup cheddar cheese
- ½ cup green onions
- Salt and pepper

INSTRUCTIONS

1. Wash and bake potatoes in oven at 400° for 1 hour.

2. In a medium bowl, combine Parmesan cheese, garlic, paprika, cheddar cheese, bacon, green onions, salt, and pepper. Mix well.

3. Remove the potatoes from the oven and allow to cool for 15 minutes. Cut lengthwise, spoon out the flesh of the potatoes, leaving 1/4 of the flesh. Discard the rest or use for something else later on.

4. Brush the inside of the skins with the oil, salt, and pepper. Turn them upside down and place on a cookie sheet. Brush outside of the skins and bake cut-side down for 6 minutes. Turn cut-side up and bake an additional 6 minutes.

5. Remove the skins from the oven and stuff with the bacon,-cheese mixture. Return them to the cookie sheet and bake an additional 3 to 4 minutes or until cheese has melted and begins to bubble.

STRAWBERRY SALSA

| PREP : 10 MINS | COOK : 1 HOUR | SERVES : 4 |

INGREDIENTS

- 1 medium tomato chopped
- ¾ cup chopped strawberries
- ¼ red onion, finely diced
- ½ jalapeno, seeded and diced
- 1/3 cup freshly chop cilantro
- 1 lime, juiced
- Salt and pepper to taste

INSTRUCTIONS

1. Combine all ingredients together in a large bowl and stir until mixed thoroughly.

2. Allow to sit for at least 1 hour. Keep in the refrigerator up to 3 days.

3. It's something light and simple. Serve with chips or over a quesadilla for a great summer dish.

SHRIMP DIP WITH SPICY CREAM CHEESE

PREP : 15 MINS | COOK : 5 MINS | SERVES : 6

INGREDIENTS

- 1 (8 ounce) pack cream cheese (room temperature)
- 1/3 cup mayonnaise
- 2 tablespoons Slap Yo' Mama Seasoning
- 1 tablespoon hot sauce
- ¼ teaspoon garlic powder
- 1/3 cup green pepper, small diced
- 1/3 cup red pepper, small diced
- 3–4-ounce cooked shrimp salad
- ½ cup green onions
- ½ teaspoon cayenne pepper

INSTRUCTIONS

1. In a large mixing bowl, mix the cream cheese, mayonnaise, Slap Yo' Mama seasoning, cayenne pepper, green onions, hot sauce, and garlic powder (using either a hand or stand mixer). Mix in the shrimp and red and green peppers for 2 mins.
2. Make sure everything is mixed well. Serve with your favorite chips or crackers.

STEAK WITH BLUE CHEESE BRUSCHETTA

PREP : 10 MINS | COOK : 10 MINS | SERVES : 6

INGREDIENTS

- 16-ounce steak, any type you like
- ¼ cup and 2 tablespoons olive oil, separated
- ½ teaspoon salt
- 1 loaf French baguette
- 6-ounce blue cheese, crumbled
- A pinch of chives

INSTRUCTIONS

1. Preheat oven to 350°. While oven preheats, prepare steak. In a medium skillet, melt the oil and butter over medium heat. Season steak with salt and pepper. Cook steak and sear 4-5 minutes per side.

2. Remove from skillet and transfer steak to a cutting board. Let rest for 10 minutes before slicing. While steak rests, make crostini.

3. Slice baguette into 1/2-inch slices on the diagonal, making about 20 toasts. Place sliced baguette on a baking sheet and brush with olive oil (about 1/4 cup for 20 slices). Top with blue cheese crumbles. Bake 4-6 minutes or until baguette is browned and cheese is melted.

4. Remove from oven, and top with a slice of steak.

SOUPS

LOBSTER BISQUE

PREP : 15 MINS | COOK : 30 MINS | SERVES : 4

INGREDIENTS

- 6 tablespoons all-purpose flour
- 6 tablespoons unsalted butter
- ½ tablespoon celery salt
- ½ teaspoon salt
- ½ teaspoon pepper
- 4 cups half-and-half
- 1 ½ cups lobster or seafood stock
- 3 cups cooked lobster meat, shredded
- 3 tablespoons tomato paste
- 3 tablespoons minced white onion
- 3 tablespoons minced celery
- 1 teaspoon paprika
- ½ teaspoon dried thyme
- ½ teaspoon seafood seasoning
- 1 cup heavy cream

INSTRUCTIONS

1. Melt butter in a large pot over medium heat. Add flour, salt, pepper, and celery salt to the pot.

2. Stir in half-and-half into the mixture, making sure you have no lumps.

3. Add lobster stock and stir. Reduce heat to low and simmer, stirring constantly, until the soup begins to thicken (about 15 minutes). Stir lobster, tomato paste, onion, and celery into the soup.

4. Season with paprika, thyme, and seafood seasoning. Continue cooking the soup (about 10 minutes). Add cream and stir. Cook about 5 minutes and serve.

CHICKEN NOODLES SOUP

PREP : 10 MINS | COOK : 30 MINS | SERVES : 4

INGREDIENTS

- ½ of onion, small chopped
- ½ cup celery, small chopped
- 4 cans of chicken broth
- 1 cooked chicken breast, small chopped
- 1 ½ cup of pasta
- 1 cup sliced carrots
- ½ teaspoon dried basil
- ½ teaspoon dried oregano
- 1 tablespoon of butter
- Salt and pepper to taste

INSTRUCTIONS

1. Melt butter in a large pot over medium heat. Add onion and celery, and cook until they're tender (about 5 minutes).
2. Add chicken broth, chicken, noodles, carrots, basil, oregano, salt, and pepper. Stir to combine. Bring to a boil and reduce heat. Simmer for 20-30 minutes. Serve.

STEAK AND POTATO SOUP

| PREP : 15 MINS | COOK : 30 MINS | SERVES : 4 |

INGREDIENTS

- 1 tablespoon olive oil
- 1 pound boneless roast, cut into cubes
- 1 cup onion, small diced
- 1 tablespoon minced garlic
- 4 cups beef stock
- 2 pounds potatoes, cubed
- ½ cup butter
- ½ cup all-purpose flour
- 3 cups milk
- 1 cup heavy cream
- 8 ounces white cheddar cheese, shredded
- Salt and pepper to taste

INSTRUCTIONS

1. Add olive oil to a pot over medium heat. Season steak with the salt and pepper, then add to the pot, stirring occasionally (about 6 to 7 minutes).

2. Remove the steak and set it aside. Leave the stock in the pot. Add the onions and garlic to the pot and cook 2 to 3 minutes until softened.

3. Pour in the beef stock and add in the potatoes. Increase the heat to high and bring to a boil. Cook for about 10-12 minutes until the potatoes are tender.

4. In a separate pot over medium heat, melt the butter. Whisk in the flour until it is well combined and add the milk.

5. Once the potatoes are fork-tender, pour in the hot milk mixture and stir until thickened (about 3-4 minutes).

6. Add the steak to the pot, along with the heavy cream, and cook until heated through (about 2-3 minutes).

7. Remove the pot from the heat and stir in the white cheddar cheese until melted. Taste and season as needed. Place in a serving bowl and enjoy.

LOADED POTATO SOUP

| PREP : 15 MINS | COOK : 30 MINS | SERVES : 4 |

INGREDIENTS

- 1 cup cooked bacon bits
- ½ onion, small diced
- 4 large Russet potatoes, diced
- ¼ cup flour
- 4 cups whole milk
- 1 cup chicken broth
- 1 clove garlic, minced
- ¾ cup cheddar cheese
- Salt & pepper to taste

INSTRUCTIONS

1. Add onion to the pot and sauté for 5 minutes on medium heat. Stir in the flour and cook for about a minute.
2. Whisk the milk in slowly until there are no clumps. Add the chicken broth, garlic, and potatoes, cooking on medium heat.
3. Cook the soup until it boils. When it begins to boil, reduce the heat and cover the pot with a lid. Let the soup simmer for 20 minutes, but keep an eye on it. Stir occasionally.
4. Stir the cheddar in the soup, then add salt and pepper to taste.

VEGETABLES

MIXED VEGETABLES
MUSHROOM, BELL PEPPERS, ONION, AND BROCCOLI WITH ITALIAN SEASONING

| PREP : 15 MINS | COOK : 30 MINS | SERVES : 4 |

INGREDIENTS

- 2 cups of mushrooms, cut in hal
- 1 red bell pepper, medium chopped
- 1 yellow bell pepper, medium chopped
- 1 green bell pepper, medium chopped
- 1 red onion, medium chopped
- 2 tablespoons olive oil
- 1 tablespoons Italian seasoning
- Salt and pepper to taste

INSTRUCTIONS

1. Preheat oven to 400°and line a baking sheet with foil.

2. Add all the vegetables to the baking sheet and pour olive oil over them.

3. Sprinkle Italian seasoning, salt, and pepper over the vegetables, and spread the vegetables out on the baking sheet.

4. Bake for 15-20 minutes, or until soft.

5. Take out of the oven, place on a serving dish, and enjoy.

CARROTS + BROWN BUTTER GARLIC SAUCE

| PREP : 15 MINS | COOK : 30 MINS | SERVES : 4 |

INGREDIENTS

Garlic brown butter:
- 3 tablespoons unsalted butter
- 1 teaspoon minced garlic
- A pinch of red pepper
- Salt and paper to taste

- 4 pounds carrots
- 1 tablespoon olive oil

INSTRUCTIONS

1. Pour the olive oil on a sheet pan and place the carrots on top. Season the carrots with salt and pepper. Roast in the oven on 400° until they are tender (about 15 minutes).

2. Add butter to a small saucepan on medium heat and allow it to simmer. Once the butter turns brown, turn off the heat, add garlic and allow it to sit for 2 minutes.

3. Pour the sauce over the carrots and enjoy!

MIXED VEGETABLES
BELL PEPPERS, ONION, AND GREEN BEANS

| PREP : 15 MINS | COOK : 10 MINS | SERVES : 3 |

INGREDIENTS

- 1 green bell pepper, seeded and small diced
- 1 red bell pepper, seeded and small diced
- 1 yellow bell pepper, seeded and small diced
- 1 half yellow onion, small diced
- 1 small bag frozen beans, thawed
- 3 tablespoons olive oil

INSTRUCTIONS

1. Cut all vegetables up and place in a large pan.
2. Sauté on medium heat with olive oil, onions, and bell peppers. Add the green beans last. Season with salt and pepper, and sauté for 4 to 8 minutes, until tender.

Scallops with Garlic Cream

Scallops with Pomegranate

BUTTERNUT SQUASH WITH RED ONIONS

| PREP : 10 MINS | COOK : 30 MINS | SERVES : 3 |

INGREDIENTS

- 3 cups peeled, sliced butternut squash
- 2 cups red onions, medium diced
- 1 tablespoon olive oil
- Salt and pepper to taste

INSTRUCTIONS

1. Toss squash, onions, salt, and pepper with olive oil in a large bowl. Place on a baking sheet and cook at 400°for 15-20 minutes until squash is tender.

2. Remove from the oven and allow to cool for 5 minutes. Place in a serving dish, serve, and enjoy.

VEGETABLE MEDLEY

| PREP : 15 MINS | COOK : 30 MINS | SERVES : 4 |

INGREDIENTS

- 1 pound brussels sprouts, halved (lengthwise)
- 4 medium carrots, cut into 2-inch chunks
- 1 half white onion, small diced
- 1 cup Italian dressing
- 2 cups cherry tomatoes
- ¼ cup olive oil
- Salt and pepper to taste

INSTRUCTIONS

1. Cut all vegetables according to instructions. In a medium pan on medium heat, sauté the onions, carrots, and brussel sprouts in olive oil for 4 to 7 minutes.

2. Cook until vegetables are tender. Add in cherry tomatoes and stir. Turn off the heat and allow the vegetables to cool for 5 minutes.

3. Add the Italian dressing, place in a serving dish, and enjoy.

SQUASH, ZUCCHINI AND GREEN ONIONS

| PREP : 10 MINS | COOK : 5 MINS | SERVES : 3 |

INGREDIENTS

- 1 zucchini, small diced
- 1 squash, small diced
- 1 cup of green onions, small sliced
- ½ cup olive oil
- Salt and pepper to taste

INSTRUCTIONS

1. Cut vegetables according to instructions above.
2. In a medium skillet on medium heat, sauté the zucchini and squash. Add in salt and pepper, and sauté for another 4-5 mins until soft.
3. Now, add in green onions and stir occasionally.
4. Turn off heat, place in a serving dish, and serve immediately.

DESSERTS

FRUIT TART

| PREP : 15 MINS | COOK : 30 MINS | SERVES : 8 |

INGREDIENTS

- 1 graham cracker crust (pre-made, 9 inch)
- 1 (8 ounce) package cream cheese, softened
- ¾ cup heavy whipping cream
- ½ cup confectioners' sugar
- 1 teaspoon vanilla extract
- 1 tablespoon condensed milk
- Fruit topping:
- 1 pint strawberries slice
- 1 pint raspberries
- 1 pint blueberries

INSTRUCTIONS

1. Bake the graham cracker crust according to the instructions on the package. Cool for 15 minutes after it comes out of the oven.

2. **Prepare the filling:**
   In your stand mixer with the whisk attachment, beat the whipped cream and vanilla until stiff peaks form. Set it aside.

3. With your mixer and the paddle attachment, mix cream cheese, confectioner sugar, and condensed milk until smooth.

4. Fold in whipped cream into cream cheese mixture but do not mix it too much.

5. **To assemble the tart:**
   Spread the filling into the graham cracker crust and top with fresh berries. Chill for an hour before slicing and serving.

BANANA PUDDING CHEESECAKE

PREP : 10 MINS | COOK : 4 HOURS | SERVES : 8

INGREDIENTS

- 1 pound Nilla Wafers
- 1 graham cracker crust (pre-made, 9 inch)
- 1 package vanilla instant pudding mix
- 1 cup whole milk
- 1 (8 ounce) package cream cheese, softened
- 1/3 cup white sugar
- 2 cup heavy whipping cream
- 1 teaspoon vanilla extract
- 2 bananas, sliced
- 4 ounces Cool Whip

INSTRUCTIONS

1. In a mixing bowl, beat vanilla instant pudding, whole milk and 1 cup of heavy cream. Once fully mixed and stiff, set aside.

2. In another bowl, beat the sugar, cream cheese, vanilla extract, and heavy cream until smooth. Mix until it's a medium stiff peak.

3. With a spatula, fold the pudding mixture into the cream cheese mixture. Pour half of the cheesecake mixture into the 9-inch graham cracker crust and top with some of the bananas.

4. Pour the remaining cheesecake mixture on top of the bananas and top the entire pie with Cool Whip.

5. Cover and chill for 4 hours.

6. Just before serving, add the Nilla wafers and remaining sliced bananas on top of the cheesecake.

TURTLE CHOCOLATE CARAMEL CHEESECAKE

PREP : 10 MINS | COOK : 4 HOURS | SERVES : 8

INGREDIENTS

- 1 pack Oreo cookies
- 9-inch pie crust, no bake

Filling:

- 1 (8 ounce) package cream cheese, softened
- 1 1/3 cups powdered sugar
- 1 ½ cups heavy cream
- ¾ cup caramel (homemade or store bought)

INSTRUCTIONS

1. **Filling:**
   Mix the cream cheese and sugar together until light and fluffy. Add in the caramel until smooth.
2. In a separate bowl, whip heavy cream until soft peaks form. Then fold into the caramel filling.
3. Spread the filling into the prepared Oreo crust and chill about 4 hours.
4. Garnish top with toasted pecan halves, hot fudge, caramel, and whipped cream.

Chocolate Turtle Cheesecake topped with Chocolate Covered Strawberries

Fruit Tart

HOMEMADE MINT OREO ICE CREAM

| PREP : 10 MINS | COOK : 5 HOURS | SERVES : 8 |

INGREDIENTS

- 2 cups heavy cream
- 1 ½ cup granulated sugar
- 1/8 teaspoon salt
- 2 tablespoons condensed milk
- 1-ounce fresh mint leaves, rinsed & finely chopped (no stems)

- 1 cup whole milk
- 1 teaspoon vanilla extract
- ½ teaspoon mint extract
- 3 drops green food coloring
- 10 Oreos, finely crushed

INSTRUCTIONS

1. In a stand mixer, mix the whole milk, condensed milk, heavy cream, sugar, vanilla, salt, mint extract, and food coloring for 2 to 8 minutes on medium speed (until the mix becomes a firm peak).

2. Now whisk in Oreos for 30 seconds.

3. Pour mixture into 2 cold metal loaf pans and freeze, covered, for up 5 hours.

HOMEMADE TIRAMISU GELATO

PREP : 10 MINS | COOK : 3 HOURS | SERVES : 6

INGREDIENTS

- ¼ cup strong coffee
- ½ cup milk
- 4 tablespoons granulated sugar
- 1 cup mascarpone
- 1 ¼ cups heavy cream
- 4-5 Lady Fingers cookies cut into small cubes

INSTRUCTIONS

1. In a mixing bowl, add cold coffee, milk, sugar, heavy cream, and mascarpone. Beat. Stir until smooth. Add lady fingers and stir. Freeze for 2-3 hours, or until firm.

APPLE PECAN BREAD PUDDING

PREP : 15 MINS | COOK : 1 HOUR | SERVES : 8

INGREDIENTS

- 8 cups bread, cut into 1-inch cubes
- 5 cups whole milk
- 1 cup heavy cream
- 4 eggs
- 2 cup sugar
- 2 tsp vanilla
- 1/2 tsp cinnamon
- 1 cup pecans, finely chopped
- 4 Granny Smith apples (peeled and cut into small chunks)
- 1 ½ cups water
- ¾ cup sugar
- ¼ cup cornstarch
- 1 teaspoon cinnamon

INSTRUCTIONS

1. Preheat oven to 350°. Spread butter on a baking dish and place bread inside the dish.
2. In a medium mixing bowl, whisk eggs, heavy cream, sugar, vanilla, and cinnamon. Whisk until all ingredients are combined.
3. Pour egg mixture over bread and let sit for 5 minutes.
4. In a small saucepan, add the apples, water, sugar, cornstarch, and cinnamon, and cook on medium heat for 5 -10 minutes. Stir constantly until the sauce thickens.
5. Add the mixture on top of the bread pudding. Place in the oven for 60 minutes.
6. Place a fork in the middle to check if it is done and if not, cook for an additional 6 minutes.
7. Take out of the oven and spread the chopped pecans on top of the bread pudding. Cut and serve. Can be served with your favorite ice cream.

SALADS

PASTA SALAD

| PREP : 5 MINS | COOK : 40 MINS | SERVES : 8 |

INGREDIENTS

- 1 pound dried pasta
- 1 cup sliced red bell pepper
- 1 can black olives (halved)
- 1 cup cherry tomatoes (halved)
- ½ red onion, thinly sliced
- 1 cup cubed ham
- 1 cucumber, small diced
- 1 cup mini pepperonis
- 1 cup Parmesan cheese
- 2 tablespoons Italian seasoning
- Salt and pepper to taste

INSTRUCTIONS

1. Cook 1 pound of pasta according to package. Allow pasta to cool completely.

2. In a large bowl, add all ingredients to the pasta and mix well.

3. Place in a serving bowl, cover, and refrigerate for 30 minutes.

GREEK SALAD

| PREP : 10 MINS | COOK : 10 MINS | SERVES : 6 |

INGREDIENTS

- 1 cucumber, small diced
- 1 pint grape tomatoes (halved)
- ½ red onion, thinly sliced
- ½ cup Kalamata olives (halved)
- 1 cup feta cheese, crumbled
- 1 green bell pepper, small diced
- ½ teaspoon dried oregano
- Salt and pepper to taste
- A pinch dried dill
- 6 tablespoons olive oil

INSTRUCTIONS

1. On a large platter, arrange the cucumbers, green peppers, cherry tomatoes, red onions, and olives. Drizzle with olive oil and toss gently. Sprinkle with oregano, salt, pepper, dill, and feta crumbles on top.

FRUIT SALAD

PREP : 10 MINS | COOK : 10 MINS | SERVES : 6

INGREDIENTS

- 3 cups strawberries, halved
- 3 cups blackberries
- 3 cups blueberries
- 2 cups kiwi, peeled and small diced
- 3 cups pineapple, peeled and small diced
- 2 cups red seedless grapes
- ½ cup honey

INSTRUCTIONS

1. Toss all fruit together in a large bowl with honey. Serve immediately.

Surf & Turf with Corn Veggie Mix

Belgian Waffle topped with Strawberry Banana

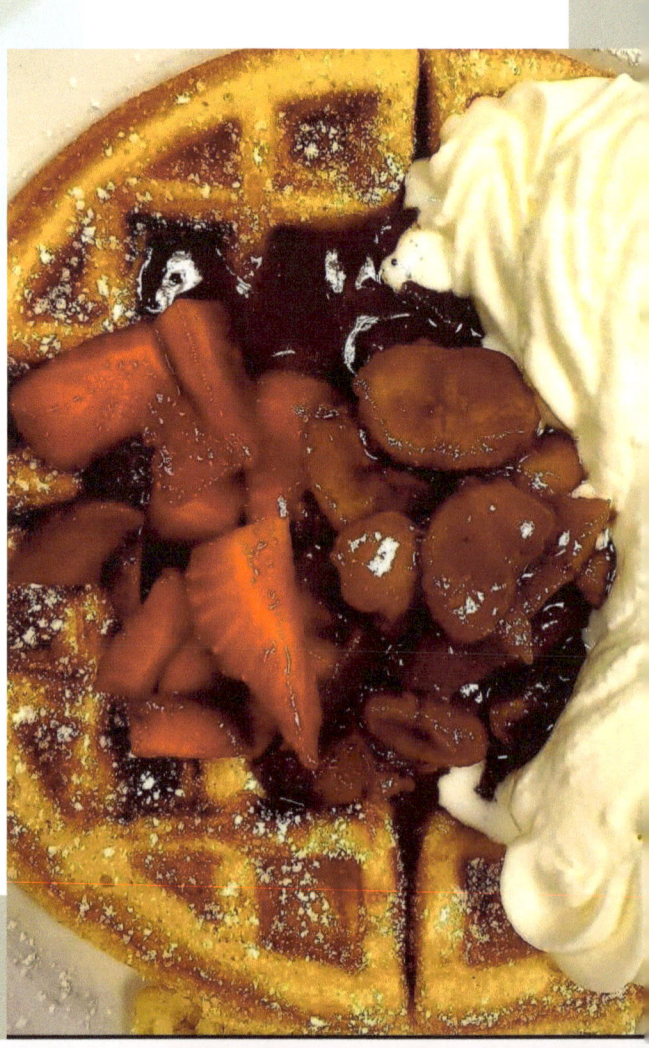

CAPRESE SALAD

| PREP : 10 MINS | COOK : 10 MINS | SERVES : 6 |

INGREDIENTS

- 1 pint grape tomatoes, cut in half
- 8 ounces mozzarella pearls
- 1 teaspoon dried basil
- 1 tablespoon olive oil
- 1 tablespoon balsamic vinegar
- Salt and pepper to taste

INSTRUCTIONS

1. In a medium bowl, add tomatoes, cheese, and basil. Next, add olive oil and balsamic vinegar. Toss together gently. Add salt and pepper to liking.

POTATO SALAD

PREP : 10 MINS | COOK : 10 MINS | SERVES : 8

INGREDIENTS

- 3 pounds potatoes, peeled
- 1 tablespoon salt
- 1 ½ cup mayonnaise
- 2 tablespoons granulated sugar
- 1 tablespoon yellow mustard
- 6 hard-boiled eggs, peeled and chopped
- 1 tablespoon white vinegar
- A pinch smoked paprika
- A pinch of pepper

INSTRUCTIONS

1. In a large pot on medium heat, cook the potatoes. Make sure the water is covering the potatoes. Add 1 tablespoon of salt. Bring potatoes to a boil, reduce heat and simmer until potatoes are tender.

2. Drain potatoes.

3. In a large bowl, whisk the mayonnaise, sugar, vinegar, and mustard. Add in the potatoes and chopped eggs. Stir to combine all ingredients.

4. Place in a serving dish, sprinkle paprika on top, and serve.

VEGAN DISHES

VEGAN CHILI

| PREP : 15 MINS | COOK : 30 MINS | SERVES : 8 |

INGREDIENTS

- 1 small yellow onion, diced
- 1 green bell pepper, seeded
- 1 cup of celery, diced
- 1 teaspoon minced garlic
- 3 small carrots, thinly sliced
- 4 tablespoons ancho chili powder
- 1 tablespoon ground cumin
- 1 teaspoon dried oregano
- ½ teaspoon cayenne pepper
- 2 small cans black beans, drained
- 2 small cans crushed tomatoes
- 1 cup low sodium vegetable broth
- Salt and pepper to taste

INSTRUCTIONS

1. Add 1/3 cup of water, onion, celery, and green pepper to a large pot, and cook on medium heat. Stir occasionally, until all the water evaporates.

2. Once the pot is dry and the vegetables start to turn golden brown, deglaze the pot with an additional ¼ cup of water. Reduce to medium heat, and add the garlic, carrots, chili powder, cumin, oregano, salt, pepper, and cayenne pepper. Sauté for 2-3 minutes, adding a small splash of water.

3. Next, add the black beans, crushed tomatoes, and the vegetable broth to the pot. Bring everything to a boil over high heat, then reduce the heat to create a simmer. Cover and cook for 10 minutes.

4. Remove the lid from the pot and cook uncovered for 5-7 additional minutes, until the carrots are tender, and the chili reaches your desired thickness.

5. Stir this mixture occasionally to make sure it doesn't stick.

6. Place the chili in a bowl and serve. It can be topped with green onions and vegan sour cream.

VEGAN FAJITAS

| PREP : 10 MINS | COOK : 30 MINS | SERVES : 8 |

INGREDIENTS

- 1 half white onion, thinly sliced
- 1 half red onion, thinly sliced
- 1 green bell pepper, seeded and thinly sliced
- 1 half cauliflower, cut into small pieces
- 1 portobello mushroom, bite-sized pieces
- 3 tablespoons olive oil
- 1 tablespoon chili powder
- 1 teaspoon cumin
- 1 teaspoon smoked paprika
- 1 teaspoon garlic powder
- 1 teaspoon onion powder
- 1 package flour tortilla
- Salt and pepper to taste

INSTRUCTIONS

1. Cut all vegetables accordingly, and mix in a large bowl with chili powder, cumin, paprika, olive oil, garlic powder, salt, and pepper.

2. Spread the vegetables out on a greased baking pan and bake for 30 minutes at 370°, or until all vegetables are soft and tender.

3. When vegetables are ready, take them out the oven and place to the side. Warm tortillas to your liking.

4. Place the vegetables inside the warm tortillas. Can be served with avocado and vegan sour cream.

SWEET POTATO CURRY

PREP : 5 MINS | COOK : 20 MINS | SERVES : 6

INGREDIENTS

- 1 tablespoon coconut oil
- 1 teaspoon minced ginger
- 1 tablespoon minced garlic
- 3 tablespoons vegan Thai red curry paste
- 2 sweet potatoes, peeled and cut into small cubes
- 1 can chickpeas, drained and rinsed
- 1 can coconut milk
- 1 cup water
- 1 small bag baby spinach
- Salt and pepper to taste

INSTRUCTIONS

1. Heat the coconut oil in a skillet over medium heat. Add the ginger and garlic, and stir for about 1 minute. Stir in the curry paste and sauté for another minute.

2. Add the sweet potatoes, chickpeas, coconut milk, water, salt, and pepper, and stir to combine. Bring the mixture to a simmer, cover, and cook until the sweet potatoes are tender (about 15-20 minutes).

3. Add the spinach and stir. Cook until the spinach wilts, then remove from heat. Curry can be served with rice.

VEGAN BIG MAC

PREP : 10 MINS | COOK : 20 MINS | SERVES : 3

INGREDIENTS

- 3 Beyond Meat patties
- 1 large sesame seed hamburger bun
- ½ small onion, minced
- 1 cup iceberg lettuce, shredded
- 3 vegan American cheese slices
- 6 sweet pickle slices

Vegan special sauce:
- 1 cup vegan mayo
- ¼ cup ketchup
- 1 ½ tablespoons mustard
- 2 teaspoons sweet pickle relish
- ½ tablespoon adobo seasoning

INSTRUCTIONS

1. In a small bowl, mix the ingredients for the special sauce. Cook burger patties according to packaging instructions.
2. While the burger is cooking, chop your onions, lettuce, and pickles. Cut the bun into three even slices. Lightly toast all three bun parts by tossing them on the heated grill pan, each side for 30 seconds, until golden brown.
3. Place the patty on the bun and spread 1 tablespoon of the special sauce. Add onion, lettuce, pickles, and cheese slices on the burger patties. Enjoy.

Ribeye Steak with Caramelized Onions, Asparagus & Scalloped Potatoes

Sauteed Shrimp with a Garlic Cream Sauce & Orzo Pasta

VEGAN STIR FRY

| PREP : 10 MINS | COOK : 5 MINS | SERVES : 6 |

INGREDIENTS

- 1 tablespoon olive oil
- ½ red onion, sliced
- 1 red bell pepper, sliced
- 1 yellow bell pepper, sliced
- 1 cup portobello mushrooms, sliced
- 1 cup carrots, sliced
- A pinch of black and white sesame seeds
- 2 cups broccoli
- 1 cup baby corn
- 2 tablespoons soy sauce
- 1 tablespoon maple syrup
- Pinch minced garlic
- 1 cup sugar snap peas
- Salt and pepper to taste

INSTRUCTIONS

1. Heat the olive oil in a wok or pan. Add the vegetables, red bell pepper, yellow bell pepper, carrot, snap peas, broccoli, onion, and mushroom. Cook over high heat for 1-4 minutes, stirring continuously. Season to taste.
2. Add the soy sauce and maple syrup, and cook for 1-2 minutes, stirring occasionally.
3. Remove from heat. Stir fry can be served over brown rice.

VEGAN BREAKFAST CASSEROLE

| PREP : 10 MINS | COOK : 40 MINS | SERVES : 6 |

INGREDIENTS

- 2 tablespoons oil, separated
- 8 mushrooms, sliced
- 1 teaspoon minced garlic
- ½ red onion, diced
- 1 half red bell pepper, small diced
- 1 half green bell pepper, small diced
- 2 cups baby spinach, chopped
- 1 cup shredded vegan cheese
- Salt and pepper to taste

INSTRUCTIONS

1. In a large skillet over medium heat, heat 1 tablespoon of the oil. Add the mushrooms, onions, and bell peppers. Sauté them for 4 minutes or until they turn brown.

2. Add a small pinch of salt, pepper, and garlic. Let cook for 2 minutes. Remove and place in a bowl.

3. Add the second tablespoon of oil and sauté the spinach. When done, remove from heat and set aside.

4. Spray a baking dish with nonstick cooking spray. Evenly spread all the mixed vegetables on the bottom of the dish.

5. Bake the casserole, uncovered, for 15-25 minutes on 375°.

6. Remove the casserole from the oven and allow it to cook for 10 minutes. Once done, add cheese and allow it to melt. Slice and enjoy.

JUST FOR KIDS

CHICKEN ALFREDO

PREP : 10 MINS | COOK : 30 MINS | SERVES : 4

INGREDIENTS

- 2 tablespoons olive oil
- 2 diced chicken breasts
- ½ teaspoon minced garlic
- 4 cups water
- 1 carton heavy cream
- 1 pound penne pasta
- 1/2 cup chicken stock
- 1 ½ cups Parmesan cheese
- Salt and pepper

INSTRUCTIONS

1. Season chicken on both sides with salt and pepper. Pour the olive oil in a pan and heat on medium heat. Add the chicken and cook until it's golden.

2. Pour water, cream, pasta, garlic, and chicken stock into the frying pan and bring to a boil. Reduce the heat to simmer and cook until the pasta is done. Stir occasionally so the pasta doesn't stick together. Season according to taste.

3. Add grated Parmesan to the pasta mix. Stir consistently so the sauce won't burn. Make sure your sauce is covering all the chicken and pasta.

4. When done, place in a serving bowl. Sprinkle Parmesan cheese on top and enjoy.

CHEESEBURGER CASSEROLE

PREP : 10 MINS | COOK : 20 MINS | SERVES : 6

INGREDIENTS

- ½ block Velveeta cheese, cut in cubes
- 1 pound ground Beef
- ½ white onion, chopped
- 2 tablespoons tomato paste
- 4 cups beef broth
- 1 pound elbow macaroni
- ½ cup whole milk
- Salt and pepper

INSTRUCTIONS

1. In a medium bowl, season the ground beef and onions with the desired amount of salt and pepper.

2. In a large pot over medium heat, cook the ground beef for about 10 minutes or until brown and crumbled. Drain any excess grease.

3. Stir in the tomato paste. Add the beef broth and the uncooked macaroni. Stir to combine. Bring to a gentle simmer over medium heat.

4. Cover the pot and let it cook for 5 minutes. Uncover, stir briefly, replace the cover, and cook for 5 more minutes. Reduce the heat to low.

5. Stir in the milk (should be room temperature) and add the Velveeta.

6. Replace the lid and heat for an additional 2-3 minutes, until the cheese is melted. Serve and enjoy.

HONEY HOT WINGS

| PREP : 10 MINS | COOK : 1 HOUR | SERVES : 4 |

INGREDIENTS

- ½ cup unsalted butter, melted
- 1 cup honey, room temperature
- 1 cup buffalo sauce
- 20 chicken wings

INSTRUCTIONS

1. Season the chicken to your liking. Place them on a greased baking sheet and place in the oven at 400°. Bake for 45-50 minutes or until a crisp golden brown. When the chicken is done, drain the grease and place in a bowl.

2. Place the melted butter, honey, and buffalo sauce in a large bowl and mix well.

3. Pour the sauce over the chicken and toss together. Place the sauced wings on the baking sheet and place under broiler at 500° for 2-4 minutes. Be sure to keep an eye on them so they won't burn.

4. When done, let it sit for 2 minutes and serve with ranch or blue cheese.

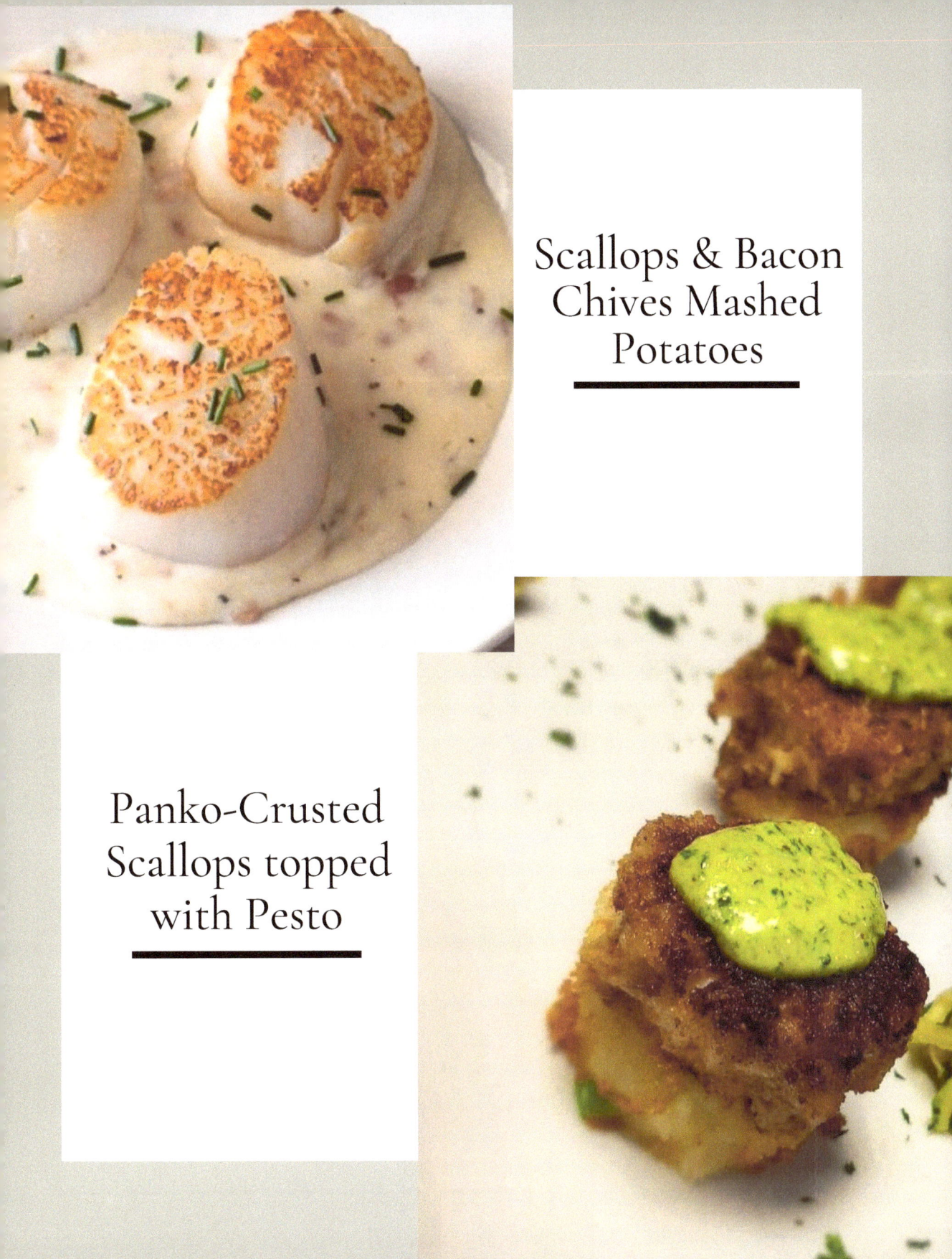

Scallops & Bacon Chives Mashed Potatoes

Panko-Crusted Scallops topped with Pesto

PIZZA BREAD

| PREP : 5 MINS | COOK : 10 MINS | SERVES : 4 |

INGREDIENTS

- 4 slices sourdough sandwich bread, toasted
- 1 cup pizza sauce
- 2 cups grated mozzarella cheese
- 16 slices pepperoni
- ½ teaspoon Italian seasoning

INSTRUCTIONS

1. Preheat oven to 375°. Place toasted bread on a baking sheet and spread the pizza sauce over the entire bread.
2. Sprinkle mozzarella cheese over the bread and place the sliced pepperoni on top. Top it off with a pinch of Italian seasoning.
3. Place in the oven and cook for 4-8 minutes, or until cheese has melted.
4. When done, take out of the oven, let sit for 1 minute, and serve.

FRUIT KABOBS

PREP : 10 MINS | COOK : 10 MINS | SERVES : 6

INGREDIENTS

- 6 strawberries
- 6 chunks cantaloupe melon
- 6 pineapple chunks
- Seedless grapes (red or green)
- Mandarin orange slices
- 6 wooden kabob skewers

INSTRUCTIONS

1. Wash and cut all fruit. Place fruit on skewer in the following order: grape, strawberry, orange, pineapple, and cantaloupe melon.
2. Repeat for all skewers.
3. Serve and enjoy.

CHICKEN AND WAFFLES

| PREP : 15 MINS | COOK : 30 MINS | SERVES : 8 |

INGREDIENTS

- 8 frozen waffles
- 8 chicken tenders (seasoned to taste)
- 4 eggs
- 2 cups all-purpose flour
- 1 bottle of your favorite syrup
- 1 quart peanut oil
- ½ cup buttermilk

INSTRUCTIONS

1. In a medium bowl, whisk the eggs and buttermilk, and add a pinch of salt and pepper.

2. Place the seasoned chicken in a large bowl, and pour the egg and buttermilk over it.

3. Pour the flour into a paper bag. Take the chicken out of the mixture and place into the flour. Shake the bag to coat the chicken.

4. Place the breaded chicken on a plate, spreading them (do not stack). Let the chicken rest for 20 minutes to allow the coating to set.

5. Heat about 3 inches of oil in a deep fryer on medium heat. In small batches, fry the chicken 5-8 minutes, or until golden brown.

6. Remove the chicken from the grease and place on a paper towel. Set aside.

7. To assemble, place the waffles on a plate and top each waffle with a chicken tender. Drizzle your favorite syrup and enjoy.

CAT FOOD

CHICKEN LIVER AND SALMON

PREP : 15 MINS | COOK : 45 MINS

INGREDIENTS

- 1 pound chicken liver
- 2 cups water
- 14 oz of wild caught salmon

INSTRUCTIONS

1. In a medium pan, cook salmon in the oven on 350° for 20 minutes.

2. In a separate pan, cook the chicken liver in the oven on 350° for 20 minutes.

3. When all the proteins are done, allow them to sit for 5 minutes to cool down. Add all the proteins to a blender with water and blend for 3 minutes. Add more water as needed to create a puree.

** Please make sure the food is free of bones. Liver must be cooked thoroughly.

** Cats cannot have too much liver because it causes vitamin A toxicity.

** Can be froze up to 2 months.

BEEF AND RICE

PREP : 30 MINS | COOK : 15 MINS

INGREDIENTS

- 4 cups ground beef
- 2 cups cooked brown rice
- 1 cup cottage cheese

INSTRUCTIONS

1. In a medium pan, cook the ground beef on medium heat. Make sure ground beef is cooked thoroughly. Once it's done, drain.
2. Blend ground beef, rice, and cheese in a blender for 2 minutes to make sure everything is blended well.

** You can add their vitamins or medicines to this mix if needed.

** Can be froze up to 2 months.

Rainbow Trout served over Goat Cheese Grits topped with Lobster, finished with Brown Butter

Seabass finished with a Champagne Butter Sauce topped with Crabmeat, over Asparagus

TUNA AND OATMEAL

PREP : 10 MINS | COOK : 20 MINS

INGREDIENTS

- 1 can tuna
- 1 ½ cup oatmeal

INSTRUCTIONS

1. Boil the oatmeal. Do not add seasoning. Allow to cool for 5 minutes.

2. Blend the tuna and oatmeal for 2 minutes, adding the juice from the tuna.

*** You can add in their medicines or vitamins.

*** Never overfeed them canned tuna or fresh tuna; it can harm them.

*** Never overfeed them canned tuna or fresh tuna; it can harm them.

HOUSEMADE CAT NIP

PREP : 10 MINS | COOK : 20 MINS

INGREDIENTS

- 1 (2 ounce) can tuna
- 2 egg whites
- 1 teaspoon dried catnip
- Parchment paper

INSTRUCTIONS

1. In a large bowl, beat 1 egg white with an electric mixer on high speed, until a stiff peak forms.

2. In a blender, combine tuna, remaining egg white, and catnip. Blend until completely smooth. Fold tuna mixture into the remaining egg white until it is combined.

3. Line a baking sheet with parchment paper. Transfer the mixture to a piping bag and pipe 1-inch rounds onto baking sheet. Bake for 20 to 25 minutes, or until dried and treats easily release from the parchment paper.

4. Cool treats completely before storing or feeding to cat. Store in an airtight container in the refrigerator for up to one month.

DOG FOOD

CHICKEN AND RICE

PREP : 15 MINS | COOK : 20 MINS

INGREDIENTS

- 4 cups cooked chicken
- 4 cups cooked white rice
- 1 cup cooked and diced carrots

INSTRUCTIONS

1. Mix in a medium bowl. Allow to cool for 5 minutes and serve.
2. Can be froze up to 1 months.

*** Never give your dog raw chicken or add any seasoning to their food. No garlic or onions.

BEEF AND BROCCOLI

PREP : 10 MINS | COOK : 15 MINS

INGREDIENTS

- 1 pound ground beef (lean; cooked all the way through with no seasoning)
- 2 cups cooked broccoli, bite sized

INSTRUCTIONS

1. Mix in a medium bowl. Allow to cool for 5 minutes and serve. Can be covered and refrigerated up to 3 days. Do not freeze.

*** Never give your dog raw chicken or add any seasoning to their food. No garlic or onions.

*** Don't add any seasoning to your fur baby's food. It's not good for them.

Ribeye topped with Garlic Cream Sauce & Crabmeat served with a Stuffed Bell Pepper & Duchess Potatoes

CARROTS AND TURKEY

PREP : 15 MINS | COOK : 15 MINS

INGREDIENTS

- 1 tablespoon coconut oil
- 1 pound ground turkey
- 2 cups carrots, small diced and cooked
- 3 cups cooked brown rice

INSTRUCTIONS

1. In a medium pan, cook ground turkey in coconut oil on medium heat. Drain all the grease from the turkey.

2. In a large bowl, add turkey, rice, and carrots. Mix with a spoon.

3. Allow to cool for 5 minutes and serve.

*** Can be refrigerated up to 3 days.

*** Never give your fur baby turkey bones or the skin of the turkey.

*** You can always add your fur baby's vitamins or medicines to this mixture.

*** Can be froze up to 1 months.

*** Don't add any seasoning to your fur baby's food. It's not good for them.

HOMEMADE SURF AND TURF

PREP : 15 MINS | COOK : 15 MINS

INGREDIENTS

- 1 tablespoon coconut oil
- 2 cups lean ground beef
- 2 cups canned tuna, drained
- 1 cup small diced sweet potatoes, cooked
- 1 cup broccoli, cut small
- 1 cup cooked white rice

INSTRUCTIONS

1. In a medium pan, cook the ground beef in the coconut oil on medium heat. When meat is done, drain.

2. In a large bowl, combine ground beef, drained tuna, broccoli, sweet potatoes, and rice. Mix well with a spoon.

3. Keep covered in the refrigerator for up to 4 days.

*** Don't add any seasoning to your fur baby's food. It's not good for them.

BAKED TREAT

PREP : 20 MINS | COOK : 15 MINS

INGREDIENTS

- 1 cup wheat flour
- ¼ cup peanut butter (all natural peanuts)
- ¼ cup mashed sweet potato

INSTRUCTIONS

1. Preheat your oven to 400°. Place a sheet of parchment paper on a baking tray.

2. Mix the flour, mashed sweet potato and peanut butter until it forms a dough. If the dough is too dry, add a splash of water. If the dough is too sticky, roll it out or add more flour. Cut your treats using a dog-shaped cookie cutter.

3. Place the treats in the oven and bake for 10-15 minutes.

*** Can be stored in an airtight container for 1 week in the refrigerator or 2 months in the freezer.

*** Don't add any seasoning to your fur baby's food. It's not good for them.

GROCERY LIST

PRODUCE

- ☐ _____
- ☐ _____
- ☐ _____
- ☐ _____
- ☐ _____
- ☐ _____
- ☐ _____
- ☐ _____
- ☐ _____

DAIRY

- ☐ _____
- ☐ _____
- ☐ _____
- ☐ _____
- ☐ _____
- ☐ _____
- ☐ _____
- ☐ _____
- ☐ _____

CANNED GOODS

- ☐ _____
- ☐ _____
- ☐ _____
- ☐ _____
- ☐ _____
- ☐ _____
- ☐ _____
- ☐ _____
- ☐ _____

FROZEN

- ☐ _____
- ☐ _____
- ☐ _____
- ☐ _____
- ☐ _____
- ☐ _____
- ☐ _____
- ☐ _____
- ☐ _____

BEVERAGES

- ☐ _____
- ☐ _____
- ☐ _____
- ☐ _____
- ☐ _____
- ☐ _____
- ☐ _____
- ☐ _____
- ☐ _____

BREAD & CEREAL

- ☐ _____
- ☐ _____
- ☐ _____
- ☐ _____
- ☐ _____
- ☐ _____
- ☐ _____
- ☐ _____
- ☐ _____

POULTRY

- ☐ _____
- ☐ _____
- ☐ _____
- ☐ _____
- ☐ _____
- ☐ _____
- ☐ _____
- ☐ _____
- ☐ _____

CONDIMENTS

- ☐ _____
- ☐ _____
- ☐ _____
- ☐ _____
- ☐ _____
- ☐ _____
- ☐ _____
- ☐ _____
- ☐ _____

OTHERS

- ☐ _____
- ☐ _____
- ☐ _____
- ☐ _____
- ☐ _____
- ☐ _____
- ☐ _____
- ☐ _____
- ☐ _____

INDEX

A
adobo seasoning, 67
apple, 55

B
bacon, 11, 16, 30, 39
baking soda, 20–21
balsamic vinegar, 11, 61
bananas, 50
bay leaves, 25
beans, 18, 43, 64
beef, 19, 38, 73, 81, 87, 90
black olives, 57
blue cheese, 19, 33, 74
blueberries, 49, 59
broccoli, 14, 41, 69, 87, 90
brown rice, 69, 81, 89
brown sugar, 11
bruschetta, 33
brussels sprouts, 46
buffalo sauce, 74
buttermilk, 20–21, 78

C
canola oil, 11, 18, 20
caramel, 51
carrots, 16, 36, 42, 46, 64, 69, 86, 89
cauliflower, 65
cayenne pepper, 22, 25, 32, 64
celery, 35–36, 64
cheddar cheese, 10, 25, 30, 38–39
cheeseburger, 37, 73
cheesecake, 50–52
cherry tomatoes, 46, 57–58
chicken, 15, 36, 39, 72, 74, 78, 80, 86–87
chicken breast, 36, 72
chicken broth, 36, 39
chicken stock, 15, 72
chicken tenders, 78
chicken wings, 74
chickpeas, 66
chili, 64–65
chili powder, 64–65
chives, 16, 33, 75
cilantro, 31
cinnamon, 55
coconut milk, 66
coconut oil, 66, 89–90
coffee, 54
condensed milk, 49, 53
cottage cheese, 81
crabmeat, 27, 82, 88
crawfish tails, 24
cream cheese, 29, 32, 49–51
Creole Sauce, 15, 17
cucumber, 57–58

cumin, 64–65

E
eggs, 16, 20–23, 55, 62, 78, 84

F
fajitas, 65
fish, 13, 15, 20–21, 24, 26
French baguette, 33
fruit, 49, 52, 59, 77

G
garlic, 10–11, 14–15, 20–25, 30, 32, 38–39, 42, 44, 64–72, 86–88
garlic powder, 14, 30, 32, 65
gelato, 54
green bell pepper, 22, 41, 43, 58, 64–65, 70
green food coloring, 53
green onions, 20–21, 24–25, 30, 32, 47, 64
grits, 10, 25, 82
ground beef, 19, 73, 81, 87, 90

H
hamburger buns, 19
heavy cream, 10, 15, 20–22, 24, 35, 38, 50–51, 53–55, 72
honey, 11, 59, 74
hot sauce, 32
hot wings, 74

I
ice cream, 53, 55
Italian dressing, 46

J
jalapeno, 31

K
Kalamata olives, 58
ketchup, 67
kiwi, 59

L
Lady Fingers cookies, 54
Lamb, 11–12
lemon juice, 22–23, 25
lobster, 35, 82

M
Mahi Mahi, 15, 17
Mandarin oranges, 77
maple syrup, 69
mascarpone, 54
mayonnaise, 19, 32, 62
mint, 53
mozzarella cheese, 76
mushrooms, 29, 41, 69–70

N
Nilla Wafers, 50

O
oatmeal, 83

olive oil, 11, 14, 24–25, 30, 33, 38, 41–47, 58, 61, 65, 69, 72
onion cream cheese spread, 29
onion powder, 14, 65
oregano, 14, 25, 36, 58, 64
oreo, 51, 53

P

paprika, 14–15, 20, 25, 30, 35, 62, 65
Parmesan cheese, 20, 27, 29–30, 57, 72
parsley, 10, 29
pasta, 13–14, 18, 26, 36, 57, 68, 72
peanut butter, 91
pecan, 51, 55
penne pasta, 72
pepperoni, 57, 76
pineapple, 59, 77
pizza, 76
pizza sauce, 76
pomegranate juice, 18
potato skins, 30
potatoes, 16, 30, 38–39, 62, 66, 68, 75, 88, 90
pudding, 50, 55

R

raspberries, 49
red bell pepper, 41, 43, 57, 69–70
red onion, 31, 41, 45, 57–58, 65, 69–70
red pepper, 15, 32, 42

red seedless grapes, 59
ribeye, 27, 68, 88
rice, 12, 14–15, 18, 66, 69, 81, 86, 89–90
roma tomatoes, 15, 24

S

salmon, 14, 17, 24, 80
salsa, 31
scallops, 10, 18, 44, 75
shallots, 13, 18
shrimp, 25, 32, 37, 68
shrimp salad, 32
Slap Yo' Mama Seasoning, 32
sour cream, 19, 64–65
soy sauce, 69
spinach, 18, 66, 70
squash, 45, 47
steak, 22–23, 27, 33, 38, 68
strawberries, 31, 49, 52, 59, 77
sugar snap peas, 69
sweet potatoes, 16, 66, 90–91
syrup, 69, 78

T

thyme, 15, 35
tiramisu, 54
tortilla, 65
tuna, 83–84, 90
turkey, 89

U
unsalted butter, 10, 13, 15–16, 18, 22, 35, 42, 74

V
vegan cheese, 67, 70
vegan mayo, 67
vegetable oil, 20
vegetables, 12, 15, 40–41, 43, 46–47, 64–65, 69–70
Velveeta cheese, 73

W
Waffle iron, 16
waffles, 16, 21, 78
whipping cream, 49–50
White Fish, 13, 20, 26
white vinegar, 62
white wine, 10, 13, 18
whole milk, 16, 39, 50, 53, 55, 73
Worcestershire sauce, 25

Y
yellow bell pepper, 41, 43, 69
yellow mustard, 62
yellow onion, 24, 43, 64

Z
zucchini, 47

www.ingramcontent.com/pod-product-compliance
Lightning Source LLC
Chambersburg PA
CBHW040724060526

44119CB00083B/320